CAPE POETRY PAPERBACKS

LEONARD COHEN
POEMS 1956–1968

Leonard Cohen

POEMS 1956–1968

JONATHAN CAPE
THIRTY BEDFORD SQUARE LONDON

FIRST PUBLISHED IN GREAT BRITAIN 1969
REPRINTED 1969, 1970 (4 times), 1971 (3 times), 1972,
1973 (twice), 1974, 1976
THIS EDITION HAS BEEN ABRIDGED FROM
Selected Poems 1956–1968
© 1964, 1966, 1968, 1969 BY LEONARD COHEN

JONATHAN CAPE LTD
30 BEDFORD SQUARE, LONDON WC1

ISBN 0 224 61776 1

Printed in Great Britain by
Fletcher & Son Ltd, Norwich
and bound by
Richard Clay (The Chaucer Press) Ltd, Bungay, Suffolk

Contents

I. LET US COMPARE MYTHOLOGIES

The Song of the Hellenist   *3*
When This American Woman   *5*
Song   *6*
These Heroics   *8*
Lovers   *9*
Letter   *10*
Saint Catherine Street   *12*
Ballad   *14*
Poem   *16*
Warning   *17*

II. THE SPICE-BOX OF EARTH

A Kite Is a Victim   *21*
The Flowers That I Left in the Ground   *22*
Gift   *24*
There Are Some Men   *25*
You All in White   *26*
It Swings, Jocko   *28*
You Have the Lovers   *30*
Owning Everything   *32*
The Cuckold's Song   *34*
Celebration   *36*
As the Mist Leaves No Scar   *37*
Now of Sleeping   *38*
For Anne   *40*

III. FLOWERS FOR HITLER

What I'm Doing Here 43
The Hearth 44
The Suit 46
My Teacher Is Dying 47
For My Old Layton 49
Finally I Called 50
The Only Tourist in Havana Turns His Thoughts
    Homeward 51
The Failure of a Secular Life 53
All There Is to Know about Adolph Eichmann 54
The Bus 55
Destiny 56
Queen Victoria and Me 57
Winter Bulletin 59
The Music Crept by Us 60
Disguises 61
One of the Nights I Didn't Kill Myself 64
The Big World 65
Another Night with Telescope 66

IV. PARASITES OF HEAVEN

Here We Are at the Window 69
I See You on a Greek Mattress 70
Two Went to Sleep 71
Found Once Again Shamelessly Ignoring the
    Swans ... 72
He Was Lame 73
I Am Too Loud When You Are Gone 74
Snow Is Falling 75
Claim Me, Blood, If You Have a Story 76

In Almond Trees Lemon Trees 77
Suzanne Takes You Down 78
This Morning I Was Dressed by the Wind 80

V. NEW POEMS

You Do Not Have to Love Me 83
You Live Like a God 84
The Reason I Write 86
A Person Who Eats Meat 87
It's Good to Sit with People 88
Do Not Forget Old Friends 91

INDEX OF FIRST LINES 93

I / Let Us Compare Mythologies

THE SONG OF THE HELLENIST

(For R.K.)

Those unshadowed figures, rounded lines of men
who kneel by curling waves, amused by ornate birds—
    If that had been the ruling way,
I would have grown long hairs for the corners of my
                            mouth . . .

O cities of the Decapolis across the Jordan,
you are too great; our young men love you,
and men in high places have caused gymnasiums
to be built in Jerusalem.
    I tell you, my people, the statues are too tall.
    Beside them we are small and ugly,
    blemishes on the pedestal.

My name is Theodotus, do not call me Jonathan.
My name is Dositheus, do not call me Nathaniel.
    Call us Alexander, Demetrius, Nicanor . . .

"Have you seen my landsmen in the museums,
the brilliant scholars with the dirty fingernails,
standing before the marble gods,
    underneath the lot?"
Among straight noses, natural and carved,
I have said my clever things thought out before;
jested on the Protocols, the cause of war,
    quoted "Bleistein with a Cigar."

And in the salon that holds the city in its great window,
in the salon among the Herrenmenschen,
among the close-haired youth, I made them laugh
when the child came in:

"Come, I need you for a Passover Cake."
And I have touched their tall clean women,
thinking somehow they are unclean,
    as scaleless fish.
They have smiled quietly at me,
and with their friends—
    I wonder what they see.

O cities of the Decapolis,
call us Alexander, Demetrius, Nicanor . . .
    Dark women, soon I will not love you.
My children will boast of their ancestors at Marathon
and under the walls of Troy,
    and Athens, my chiefest joy—

O call me Alexander, Demetrius, Nicanor . . .

WHEN THIS AMERICAN WOMAN

When this American woman,
whose thighs are bound in casual red cloth,
comes thundering past my sitting-place
like a forest-burning Mongol tribe,
the city is ravished
and brittle buildings of a hundred years
splash into the street;
and my eyes are burnt
for the embroidered Chinese girls,
already old,
and so small between the thin pines
on these enormous landscapes,
that if you turn your head
they are lost for hours.

SONG

The naked weeping girl
is thinking of my name
turning my bronze name
over and over
with the thousand fingers
of her body
anointing her shoulders
with the remembered odour
of my skin

O I am the general
in her history
over the fields
driving the great horses
dressed in gold cloth
wind on my breastplate
sun in my belly

May soft birds
soft as a story to her eyes
protect her face
from my enemies
and vicious birds
whose sharp wings
were forged in metal oceans
guard her room
from my assassins

And night deal gently with her
high stars maintain the whiteness
of her uncovered flesh

And may my bronze name
touch always her thousand fingers
grow brighter with her weeping
until I am fixed like a galaxy
and memorized
in her secret and fragile skies.

THESE HEROICS

If I had a shining head
and people turned to stare at me
in the streetcars;
and I could stretch my body
through the bright water
and keep abreast of fish and water snakes;
if I could ruin my feathers
in flight before the sun;
do you think that I would remain in this room,
reciting poems to you,
and making outrageous dreams
with the smallest movements of your mouth?

LOVERS

During the first pogrom they
Met behind the ruins of their homes—
Sweet merchants trading: her love
For a history-full of poems.

And at the hot ovens they
Cunningly managed a brief
Kiss before the soldier came
To knock out her golden teeth.

And in the furnace itself
As the flames flamed higher,
He tried to kiss her burning breasts
As she burned in the fire.

Later he often wondered:
Was their barter completed?
While men around him plundered
And knew he had been cheated.

LETTER

How you murdered your family
means nothing to me
as your mouth moves across my body

And I know your dreams
of crumbling cities and galloping horses
of the sun coming too close
and the night never ending

but these mean nothing to me
beside your body

I know that outside a war is raging
that you issue orders
that babies are smothered and generals beheaded

but blood means nothing to me
it does not disturb your flesh

tasting blood on your tongue
does not shock me
as my arms grow into your hair

Do not think I do not understand
what happens
after the troops have been massacred
and the harlots put to the sword

And I write this only to rob you

that when one morning my head
hangs dripping with the other generals
from your house gate

that all this was anticipated
and so you will know that it meant nothing to me.

SAINT CATHERINE STREET

Towering black nuns frighten us
as they come lumbering down the tramway aisle
amulets and talismans caught in careful fingers
promising plagues for an imprudent glance
So we bow our places away
          the price of an indulgence

How may we be saints and live in golden coffins
Who will leave on our stone shelves
          pathetic notes for intervention
How may we be calm marble gods at ocean altars
Who will murder us for some high reason

There are no ordeals
Fire and water have passed from the wizards' hands
We cannot torture or be tortured
Our eyes are worthless to an inquisitor's heel
No prince will waste hot lead
          or build a spiked casket for us

Once with a flaming belly she danced upon a green road
Move your hand slowly through a cobweb
          and make drifting strings for puppets
Now the tambourines are dull
at her lifted skirt boys study cigarette stubs
no one is jealous of her body

We would bathe in a free river
but the lepers in some spiteful gesture
have suicided in the water

and all the swollen quiet bodies crowd the other
    prey for a fearless thief or beggar

How can we love and pray
when at our lovers' arms
we hear the damp bells of them
who once took bitter alms
but now float quietly away

Will no one carve from our bodies a white cross
for a wind-torn mountain
or was that forsaken man's pain
enough to end all passion

Are those dry faces and hands we see
all the flesh there is of nuns
Are they really clever non-excreting tapestries
prepared by skillful eunuchs
for our trembling friends

BALLAD

My lady was found mutilated
in a Mountain Street boarding house.
My lady was a tall slender love,
    like one of Tennyson's girls,
and you always imagined her erect on a thoroughbred
in someone's private forest.
    But there she was,
naked on an old bed, knife slashes
across her breasts, legs badly cut up:
Dead two days.

They promised me an early conviction.
We will eavesdrop on the adolescents
    examining pocket-book covers in drugstores.
We will note the broadest smiles at torture scenes
    in movie houses.
We will watch the old men in Dominion Square
    follow with their eyes
the secretaries from the Sun Life at five-thirty . . .

Perhaps the tabloids alarmed him.
Whoever he was the young man came alone
    to see the frightened blonde have her blouse
ripped away by anonymous hands;
the person guarded his mouth
    who saw the poker blacken the eyes
of the Roman prisoner;
the old man pretended to wind his pocket-watch . . .

The man was never discovered.
There are so many cities!
    so many knew of my lady and her beauty.

Perhaps he came from Toronto, a half-crazed man
    looking for some Sunday love;
or a vicious poet stranded too long in Winnipeg;
or a Nova Scotian fleeing from the rocks and preachers . . .

Everyone knew my lady
    from the movies and art-galleries,
Body from Goldwyn. Botticelli had drawn her long limbs.
Rossetti the full mouth.
Ingres had coloured her skin.
    She should not have walked so bravely
through the streets.
After all, that was the Marian year, the year
the rabbis emerged from their desert exile, the year
the people were inflamed by tooth-paste ads . . .

We buried her in Spring-time.
    The sparrows in the air
wept that we should hide with earth
    the face of one so fair.

The flowers they were roses
    and such sweet fragrance gave
that all my friends were lovers
    and we danced upon her grave.

POEM

I heard of a man
who says words so beautifully
that if he only speaks their name
women give themselves to him.

If I am dumb beside your body
while silence blossoms like tumors on our lips
it is because I hear a man climb stairs
and clear his throat outside our door.

WARNING

If your neighbour disappears
O if your neighbour disappears
The quiet man who raked his lawn
The girl who always took the sun

Never mention it to your wife
Never say at dinner time
Whatever happened to that man
Who used to rake his lawn

Never say to your daughter
As you're walking home from church
Funny thing about that girl
I haven't seen her for a month

And if your son says to you
Nobody lives next door
They've all gone away
Send him to bed with no supper

Because it can spread, it can spread
And one fine evening coming home
Your wife and daughter and son
They'll have caught the idea and will be gone.

II / The Spice-Box of Earth

A KITE IS A VICTIM

A kite is a victim you are sure of.
You love it because it pulls
gentle enough to call you master,
strong enough to call you fool;
because it lives
like a desperate trained falcon
in the high sweet air,
and you can always haul it down
to tame it in your drawer.

A kite is a fish you have already caught
in a pool where no fish come,
so you play him carefully and long,
and hope he won't give up,
or the wind die down.

A kite is the last poem you've written,
so you give it to the wind,
but you don't let it go
until someone finds you
something else to do.

A kite is a contract of glory
that must be made with the sun,
so you make friends with the field
the river and the wind,
then you pray the whole cold night before,
under the travelling cordless moon,
to make you worthy and lyric and pure.

THE FLOWERS THAT I LEFT
IN THE GROUND

The flowers that I left in the ground,
that I did not gather for you,
today I bring them all back,
to let them grow forever,
not in poems or marble,
but where they fell and rotted.

And the ships in their great stalls,
huge and transitory as heroes,
ships I could not captain,
today I bring them back
to let them sail forever,
not in model or ballad,
but where they were wrecked and scuttled.

And the child on whose shoulders I stand,
whose longing I purged
with public, kingly discipline,
today I bring him back
to languish forever,
not in confession or biography,
but where he flourished,
growing sly and hairy.

It is not malice that draws me away,
draws me to renunciation, betrayal:
it is weariness, I go for weariness of thee.
Gold, ivory, flesh, love, God, blood, moon—
I have become the expert of the catalogue.

My body once so familiar with glory,
my body has become a museum:
this part remembered because of someone's mouth,
this because of a hand,
this of wetness, this of heat.

Who owns anything he has not made?
With your beauty I am as uninvolved
as with horses' manes and waterfalls.
This is my last catalogue.
I breathe the breathless
I love you, I love you—
and let you move forever.

GIFT

You tell me that silence
is nearer to peace than poems
but if for my gift
I brought you silence
(for I know silence)
you would say
This is not silence
this is another poem
and you would hand it back to me.

THERE ARE SOME MEN

There are some men
who should have mountains
to bear their names to time.

Grave-markers are not high enough
or green,
and sons go far away
to lose the fist
their father's hand will always seem.

I had a friend:
he lived and died in mighty silence
and with dignity,
left no book, son, or lover to mourn.

Nor is this a mourning-song
but only a naming of this mountain
on which I walk,
fragrant, dark, and softly white
under the pale of mist.
I name this mountain after him.

YOU ALL IN WHITE

Whatever cities are brought down,
I will always bring you poems,
and the fruit of orchards
I pass by.

Strangers in your bed,
excluded by our grief,
listening to sleep-whispering,
will hear their passion beautifully explained,
and weep because they cannot kiss
your distant face.

Lovers of my beloved,
watch how my words put on her lips like clothes,
how they wear her body like a rare shawl.
Fruit is pyramided on the window-sill,
songs flutter against the disappearing wall.

The sky of the city
is washed in the fire
of Lebanese cedar and gold.
In smoky filigree cages
the apes and peacocks fret.
Now the cages do not hold,
in the burning street man and animal
perish in each other's arms,
peacocks drown around the melting throne.

Is it the king
who lies beside you listening?
Is it Solomon or David
or stuttering Charlemagne?

Is that his crown
in the suitcase beside your bed?

When we meet again,
you all in white,
I smelling of orchards,
when we meet—

But now you awaken,
and you are tired of this dream.
Turn toward the sad-eyed man.
He stayed by you all the night.
You will have something
to say to him.

IT SWINGS, JOCKO

It swings, Jocko,
but we do not want too much flesh in it.
Make it like fifteenth-century prayers,
love with no climax,
constant love,
and passion without flesh.
(Draw those out, Jocko,
like the long snake from Moses' arm;
how he must have screamed
to see a snake come out of him;
no wonder he never felt holy:
We want that scream tonight.)
Lightly, lightly,
I want to be hungry,
hungry for food,
for love, for flesh;
I want my dreams to be of deprivation,
gold thorns being drawn from my temples.
If I am hungry
then I am great,
and I love like the passionate scientist
who knows the sky
is made only of wave-lengths.
Now if you want to stand up,
stand up lightly,
we'll lightly march around the city.
I'm behind you, man,
and the streets are spread with chicks and palms,
white branches and summer arms.
We're going through on tiptoe,
like monks before the Virgin's statue.

We built the city,
we drew the water through,
we hang around the rinks,
the bars, the festive halls,
like Brueghel's men.
Hungry, hungry.
Come back, Jocko,
bring it all back for the people here,
it's your turn now.

YOU HAVE THE LOVERS

You have the lovers,
they are nameless, their histories only for each other,
and you have the room, the bed and the windows.
Pretend it is a ritual.
Unfurl the bed, bury the lovers, blacken the windows,
let them live in that house for a generation or two.
No one dares disturb them.
Visitors in the corridor tip-toe past the long closed door,
they listen for sounds, for a moan, for a song:
nothing is heard, not even breathing.
You know they are not dead,
you can feel the presence of their intense love.
Your children grow up, they leave you,
they have become soldiers and riders.
Your mate dies after a life of service.
Who knows you? Who remembers you?
But in your house a ritual is in progress:
it is not finished: it needs more people.
One day the door is opened to the lover's chamber.
The room has become a dense garden,
full of colours, smells, sounds you have never known.
The bed is smooth as a wafer of sunlight,
in the midst of the garden it stands alone.
In the bed the lovers, slowly and deliberately and silently,
perform the act of love.
Their eyes are closed,
as tightly as if heavy coins of flesh lay on them.
Their lips are bruised with new and old bruises.
Her hair and his beard are hopelessly tangled.
When he puts his mouth against her shoulder
she is uncertain whether her shoulder
has given or received the kiss.

All her flesh is like a mouth.
He carries his fingers along her waist
and feels his own waist caressed.
She holds him closer and his own arms tighten around her.
She kisses the hand beside her mouth.
It is his hand or her hand, it hardly matters,
there are so many more kisses.
You stand beside the bed, weeping with happiness,
you carefully peel away the sheets
from the slow-moving bodies.
Your eyes are filled with tears, you barely make out the
    lovers.
As you undress you sing out, and your voice is magnificent
because now you believe it is the first human voice
heard in that room.
The garments you let fall grow into vines.
You climb into bed and recover the flesh.
You close your eyes and allow them to be sewn shut.
You create an embrace and fall into it.
There is only one moment of pain or doubt
as you wonder how many multitudes are lying beside your
    body,
but a mouth kisses and a hand soothes the moment away.

OWNING EVERYTHING

For your sake I said I will praise the moon,
tell the colour of the river,
find new words for the agony
and ecstasy of gulls.

Because you are close,
everything that men make, observe
or plant is close, is mine:
the gulls slowly writhing, slowly singing
on the spears of wind;
the iron gate above the river;
the bridge holding between stone fingers
her cold bright necklace of pearls.

The branches of shore trees,
like trembling charts of rivers,
call the moon for an ally
to claim their sharp journeys
out of the dark sky,
but nothing in the sky responds.
The branches only give a sound
to miles of wind.

With your body and your speaking
you have spoken for everything,
robbed me of my strangerhood,
made me one
with the root and gull and stone,
and because I sleep so near to you
I cannot embrace
or have my private love with them.

You worry that I will leave you.
I will not leave you.
Only strangers travel.
Owning everything,
I have nowhere to go.

THE CUCKOLD'S SONG

If this looks like a poem
I might as well warn you at the beginning
that it's not meant to be one.
I don't want to turn anything into poetry.
I know all about her part in it
but I'm not concerned with that right now.
This is between you and me.
Personally I don't give a damn who led who on:
in fact I wonder if I give a damn at all.
But a man's got to say something.
Anyhow you fed her 5 McKewan Ales,
took her to your room, put the right records on,
and in an hour or two it was done.
I know all about passion and honour
but unfortunately this had really nothing to do with
        either:
oh there was passion I'm only too sure
and even a little honour
but the important thing was to cuckold Leonard Cohen.
Hell, I might just as well address this to the both of you:
I haven't time to write anything else.
I've got to say my prayers.
I've got to wait by the window.
I repeat: the important thing was to cuckold Leonard
        Cohen.
I like that line because it's got my name in it.
What really makes me sick
is that everything goes on as it went before:
I'm still a sort of friend,
I'm still a sort of lover.
But not for long:
that's why I'm telling this to the two of you.

The fact is I'm turning to gold, turning to gold.
It's a long process, they say,
it happens in stages.
This is to inform you that I've already turned to clay.

CELEBRATION

When you kneel below me
and in both your hands
hold my manhood like a sceptre,

When you wrap your tongue
about the amber jewel
and urge my blessing,

I understand those Roman girls
who danced around a shaft of stone
and kissed it till the stone was warm.

Kneel, love, a thousand feet below me,
so far I can barely see your mouth and hands
perform the ceremony,

Kneel till I topple to your back
with a groan, like those gods on the roof
that Samson pulled down.

AS THE MIST LEAVES NO SCAR

As the mist leaves no scar
On the dark green hill,
So my body leaves no scar
On you, nor ever will.

When wind and hawk encounter,
What remains to keep?
So you and I encounter,
Then turn, then fall to sleep.

As many nights endure
Without a moon or star,
So will we endure
When one is gone and far.

NOW OF SLEEPING

Under her grandmother's patchwork quilt
a calico bird's-eye view
of crops and boundaries
naming dimly the districts of her body
sleeps my Annie like a perfect lady

Like ages of weightless snow
on tiny oceans filled with light
her eyelids enclose deeply
a shade tree of birthday candles
one for every morning
until the now of sleeping

The small banner of blood
kept and flown by Brother Wind
long after the pierced bird fell down
is like her red mouth
among the squalls of pillow

Bearers of evil fancy
of dark intention and corrupting fashion
who come to rend the quilt
plough the eye and ground the mouth
will contend with mighty Mother Goose
and Farmer Brown and all good stories
of invincible belief
which surround her sleep
like the golden weather of a halo

Well-wishers and her true lover
may stay to watch my Annie
sleeping like a perfect lady

under her grandmother's patchwork quilt
but they must promise to whisper
and to vanish by morning—
all but her one true lover.

FOR ANNE

With Annie gone,
Whose eyes to compare
With the morning sun?

Not that I did compare,
But I do compare
Now that she's gone.

III / Flowers for Hitler

WHAT I'M DOING HERE

I do not know if the world has lied
I have lied
I do not know if the world has conspired against love
I have conspired against love
The atmosphere of torture is no comfort
I have tortured
Even without the mushroom cloud
still I would have hated
Listen
I would have done the same things
even if there were no death
I will not be held like a drunkard
under the cold tap of facts
I refuse the universal alibi

Like an empty telephone booth passed at night
and remembered
like mirrors in a movie palace lobby consulted
only on the way out
like a nymphomaniac who binds a thousand
into strange brotherhood
I wait
for each one of you to confess

THE HEARTH

The day wasn't exactly my own
since I checked
    and found it on a public calendar.
Tripping over many pairs of legs
as I walked down the park
    I also learned my lust
was not so rare a masterpiece.

Buildings actually built
wars planned with blood and fought
men who rose to generals
    deserved an honest thought
as I walked down the park.

I came back quietly to your house
which has a place on a street.
    Not a single other house
disappeared when I came back.
You said some suffering
    had taught me that.

I'm slow to learn I began
to speak of stars and hurricanes.
    Come here little Galileo—
you undressed my vision—
    it's happier and easier by far
or cities wouldn't be so big.

Later you worked over lace
    and I numbered many things
your fingers and all fingers did.

As if to pay me a sweet
    for my ardour on the rug
you wondered in the middle of a stitch:
Now what about those stars and hurricanes?

THE SUIT

I am locked in a very expensive suit
old elegant and enduring
Only my hair has been able to get free
but someone has been leaving
their dandruff in it
Now I will tell you
all there is to know about optimism
Each day in hubcap mirror
in soup reflection
in other people's spectacles
I check my hair
for an army of Alpinists
for Indian rope trick masters
for tangled aviators
for dove and albatross
for insect suicides
for abominable snowmen
I check my hair
for aerialists of every kind
Dedicated as an automatic elevator
I comb my hair for possibilities
I stick my neck out
I lean illegally from locomotive windows
and only for the barber
do I wear a hat

MY TEACHER IS DYING

Martha they say you are gentle
No doubt you labour at it
Why is it I see you
leaping into unmade beds
strangling the telephone
Why is it I see you
hiding your dirty nylons
in the fireplace
Martha talk to me
My teacher is dying
His laugh is already dead
that put cartilage
between the bony facts
Now they rattle loud
Martha talk to me
Mountain Street is dying
Apartment fifteen is dying
Apartment seven and eight are dying
All the rent is dying
Martha talk to me
I wanted all the dancers' bodies
to inhabit like his old classroom
where everything that happened
was tender and important
Martha talk to me
Toss out the fake Jap silence
Scream in my kitchen
logarithms laundry lists anything
Talk to me
My radio is falling to pieces
My betrayals are so fresh
they still come with explanations

Martha talk to me
What sordid parable
do you teach by sleeping
Talk to me
for my teacher is dying
The cars are parked
on both sides of the street
some facing north
some facing south
I draw no conclusions
Martha talk to me
I could burn my desk
when I think how perfect we are
you asleep me finishing
the last of the Saint Emilion
Talk to me gentle Martha
dreaming of percussions massacres
hair pinned to the ceiling
I'll keep your secret
Let's tell the milkman
we have decided
to marry our rooms

FOR MY OLD LAYTON

His pain, unowned, he left
in paragraphs of love, hidden,
like a cat leaves shit
under stones, and he crept out in day,
clean, arrogant, swift, prepared
to hunt or sleep or starve.

The town saluted him with garbage
which he interpreted as praise
for his muscular grace. Orange peels,
cans, discarded guts rained like ticker-tape.
For a while he ruined their nights
by throwing his shadow in moon-full windows
as he spied on the peace of gentle folk.

Once he envied them. Now with a happy
screech he bounded from monument to monument
in their most consecrated plots, drunk
to know how close he lived to the breathless
in the ground, drunk to feel how much he loved
the snoring mates, the old, the children of the town.

Until at last, like Timon, tired
of human smell, resenting even
his own shoe-steps in the wilderness,
he chased animals, wore live snakes, weeds
for bracelets. When the sea
pulled back the tide like a blanket
he slept on stone cribs, heavy,
dreamless, the salt-bright atmosphere
like an automatic laboratory
building crystals in his hair.

FINALLY I CALLED

Finally I called the people I didn't want to hear from
After the third ring I said
I'll let it ring five more times then what will I do
The telephone is a fine instrument
but I never learned to work it very well
Five more rings and I'll put the receiver down
I know where it goes I know that much
The telephone was black with silver rims
The booth was cozier than the drugstore
There were a lot of creams and scissors and tubes
I needed for my body
I was interested in many coughdrops
I believe the drugstore keeper hated
his telephone and people like me
who ask for change so politely
I decided to keep to the same street
and go into the fourth drugstore
and call them again

THE ONLY TOURIST IN HAVANA
TURNS HIS THOUGHTS HOMEWARD

Come, my brothers,
let us govern Canada,
let us find our serious heads,
let us dump asbestos on the White House,
let us make the French talk English,
    not only here but everywhere,
let us torture the Senate individually
    until they confess,
let us purge the New Party,
let us encourage the dark races
    so they'll be lenient
    when they take over,
let us make the CBC talk English,
let us all lean in one direction
    and float down
    to the coast of Florida,
let us have tourism,
let us flirt with the enemy,
let us smelt pig-iron in our back yards,
let us sell snow
    to under-developed nations,
(Is it true one of our national leaders
    was a Roman Catholic?)
let us terrorize Alaska,
let us unite
    Church and State,
let us not take it lying down,
let us have two Governor Generals
    at the same time,
let us have another official language,
let us determine what it will be,

let us give a Canada Council Fellowship
    to the most original suggestion,
let us teach sex in the home
    to parents,
let us threaten to join the U.S.A.
    and pull out at the last moment,
my brothers, come,
our serious heads are waiting for us somewhere
    like Gladstone bags abandoned
    after a *coup d'état,*
let us put them on very quickly,
let us maintain a stony silence
    on the St. Lawrence Seaway.

Havana
April 1961

THE FAILURE OF A SECULAR LIFE

The pain-monger came home
from a hard day's torture.

He came home with his tongs.
He put down his black bag.

His wife hit him with an open nerve
and a cry the trade never heard.

He watched her real-life Dachau,
knew his career was ruined.

Was there anything else to do?
He sold his bag and tongs,

went to pieces. A man's got to be able
to bring his wife something.

ALL THERE IS TO KNOW
ABOUT ADOLPH EICHMANN

EYES: .... Medium
HAIR: .... Medium
WEIGHT: .... Medium
HEIGHT: .... Medium
DISTINGUISHING FEATURES: .... None
NUMBER OF FINGERS: .... Ten
NUMBER OF TOES: .... Ten
INTELLIGENCE: .... Medium

What did you expect?

Talons?

Oversize incisors?

Green saliva?

Madness?

THE BUS

I was the last passenger of the day,
I was alone on the bus,
I was glad they were spending all that money
just getting me up Eighth Avenue.
Driver! I shouted, it's you and me tonight,
let's run away from this big city
to a smaller city more suitable to the heart,
let's drive past the swimming pools of Miami Beach,
you in the driver's seat, me several seats back,
but in the racial cities we'll change places
so as to show how well you've done up North,
and let us find ourselves some tiny American fishing village
in unknown Florida
and park right at the edge of the sand,
a huge bus pointing out,
metallic, painted, solitary,
with New York plates.

DESTINY

I want your warm body to disappear
politely and leave me alone in the bath
because I want to consider my destiny.
Destiny! why do you find me in this bathtub,
idle, alone, unwashed, without even
the intention of washing except at the last moment?
Why don't you find me at the top of a telephone pole,
repairing the lines from city to city?
Why don't you find me riding a horse through Cuba,
a giant of a man with a red machete?
Why don't you find me explaining machines
to underprivileged pupils, negroid Spaniards,
happy it is not a course in creative writing?
Come back here, little warm body,
it's time for another day.
Destiny has fled and I settle for you
who found me staring at you in a store
one afternoon four years ago
and slept with me every night since.
How do you find my sailor eyes after all this time?
Am I what you expected?
Are we together too much?
Did Destiny shy at the double Turkish towel,
our knowledge of each other's skin,
our love which is a proverb on the block,
our agreement that in matters spiritual
I should be the Man of Destiny
and you should be the Woman of the House?

QUEEN VICTORIA AND ME

Queen Victoria
my father and all his tobacco loved you
I love you too in all your forms
the slim unlovely virgin anyone would lay
the white figure floating among German beards
the mean governess of the huge pink maps
the solitary mourner of a prince
Queen Victoria
I am cold and rainy
I am dirty as a glass roof in a train station
I feel like an empty cast-iron exhibition
I want ornaments on everything
because my love she gone with other boys
Queen Victoria
do you have a punishment under the white lace
will you be short with her
and make her read little Bibles
will you spank her with a mechanical corset
I want her pure as power
I want her skin slightly musty with petticoats
will you wash the easy bidets out of her head
Queen Victoria
I'm not much nourished by modern love
Will you come into my life
with your sorrow and your black carriages
and your perfect memory
Queen Victoria
The 20th century belongs to you and me
Let us be two severe giants
(not less lonely for our partnership)
who discolour test tubes in the halls of science

who turn up unwelcome at every World's Fair
heavy with proverb and correction
confusing the star-dazed tourists
with our incomparable sense of loss

WINTER BULLETIN

Toronto has been good to me
I relaxed on TV
I attacked several dead horses
I spread rumours about myself
I reported a Talmudic quarrel
    with the Montreal Jewish Community
I forged a death certificate
    in case I had to disappear
I listened to a huckster
    welcome me to the world
I slept behind my new sunglasses
I abandoned the care of my pimples
I dreamed that I needed nobody
I faced my trap
I withheld my opinion on matters
    on which I had no opinion
I humoured the rare January weather
    with a jaunty step for the sake of heroism
Not very carefully
    I thought about the future
and how little I know about animals
The future seemed unnecessarily black and strong
as if it had received my casual mistakes
through a carbon sheet

THE MUSIC CREPT BY US

I would like to remind
the management
that the drinks are watered
and the hat-check girl
has syphilis
and the band is composed
of former SS monsters
However since it is
New Year's Eve
and I have lip cancer
I will place my
paper hat on my
concussion and dance

DISGUISES

I am sorry that the rich man must go
and his house become a hospital.
I loved his wine, his contemptuous servants,
his ten-year-old ceremonies.
I loved his car which he wore like a snail's shell
everywhere, and I loved his wife,
the hours she put into her skin,
the milk, the lust, the industries
that served her complexion.
I loved his son who looked British
but had American ambitions
and let the word aristocrat comfort him
like a reprieve while Kennedy reigned.
I loved the rich man: I hate to see
his season ticket for the Opera
fall into a pool for opera-lovers.

I am sorry that the old worker must go
who called me mister when I was twelve
and sir when I was twenty
who studied against me in obscure socialist
clubs which met in restaurants.
I loved the machine he knew like a wife's body.
I loved his wife who trained bankers
in an underground pantry
and never wasted her ambition in ceramics.
I loved his children who debate
and come first at McGill University.
Goodbye old gold-watch winner
all your complex loyalties
must now be borne by one-faced patriots.

Goodbye dope fiends of North Eastern Lunch
circa 1948, your spoons which were not
Swedish Stainless, were the same colour
as the hoarded clasps and hooks
of discarded soiled therapeutic corsets.
I loved your puns about snow
even if they lasted the full seven-month
Montreal winter. Go write your memoirs
for the Psychedelic Review.

Goodbye sex fiends of Beaver Pond
who dreamed of being jacked-off
by electric milking machines.
You had no Canada Council.
You had to open little boys
with a pen-knife.
I loved your statement to the press:
"I didn't think he'd mind."
Goodbye articulate monsters
Abbott and Costello have met Frankenstein.

I am sorry that the conspirators must go
the ones who scared me by showing me
a list of all the members of my family.
I loved the way they reserved judgement
about Genghis Khan. They loved me because
I told them their little beards
made them dead-ringers for Lenin.
The bombs went off in Westmount
and now they are ashamed
like a successful outspoken Schopenhauerian
whose room-mate has committed suicide.
Suddenly they are all making movies.
I have no one to buy coffee for.

I embrace the changeless:
the committed men in public wards
oblivious as Hassidim
who believe that they are someone else.
Bravo! Abelard, viva! Rockefeller,
have these buns, Napoleon,
hurrah! betrayed Duchess.
Long live you chronic self-abusers!
you monotheists!
you familiars of the Absolute
sucking at circles!
You are all my comfort
as I turn to face the beehive
as I disgrace my style
as I coarsen my nature
as I invent jokes
as I pull up my garters
as I accept responsibility.

You comfort me
incorrigible betrayers of the self
as I salute fashion
and bring my mind
    like a promiscuous air-hostess
handing out parachutes in a nose dive
bring my butchered mind
to bear upon the facts.

ONE OF THE NIGHTS I
DIDN'T KILL MYSELF

You dance on the day you saved
my theoretical angels
daughters of the new middle-class
who wear your mouths like Bardot
    Come my darlings
the movies are true
I am the lost sweet singer whose death
in the fog your new high-heeled boots
have ground into cigarette butts
I was walking the harbour this evening
looking for a 25-cent bed of water
but I will sleep tonight
with your garters curled in my shoes
like rainbows on vacation
with your virginity ruling
the condom cemeteries like a 2nd chance
I believe I believe
Thursday December 12th
is not the night
and I will kiss again the slope of a breast
little nipple above me
like a sunset

THE BIG WORLD

The big world will find out
about this farm
the big world will learn
the details of what
I worked out in the can

And your curious life with me
will be told so often
that no one will believe
you grew old

ANOTHER NIGHT WITH TELESCOPE

Come back to me
        brutal empty room
Thin Byzantine face
    preside over this new fast
I am broken with easy grace
Let me be neither
        father nor child
but one who spins
on an eternal unimportant loom
    patterns of wars and grass
which do not last the night
        I know the stars
are wild as dust
and wait for no man's discipline
        but as they wheel
from sky to sky they rake
        our lives with pins of light

IV / Parasites of Heaven

HERE WE ARE AT THE WINDOW

Here we are at the window. Great unbound sheaves of rain wandering across the mountain, parades of wind and driven silver grass. So long I've tried to give a name to freedom, today my freedom lost its name, like a student's room travelling into the morning with its lights still on. Every act has its own style of freedom, whatever that means. Now I'm commanded to think of weeds, to worship the strong weeds that grew through the night, green and wet, the white thread roots taking lottery orders from the coils of brain mud, the permeable surface of the world. Did you know that the brain developed out of a fold in the epidermis? Did you? Falling ribbons of silk, the length of rivers, cross the face of the mountain, systems of grass and cable. Freedom lost its name to the style with which things happen. The straight trees, the spools of weed, the travelling skeins of rain floating through the folds of the mountain—here we are at the window. Are you ready now? Have I dismissed myself? May I fire from the hip? Brothers, each at your window, we are the style of so much passion, we are the order of style, we are pure style called to delight a fold of the sky.

I SEE YOU ON A GREEK MATTRESS

I see you on a Greek mattress
reading the *Book of Changes*,
Lebanese candy in the air.
On the whitewashed wall I see
you raise another hexagram
for the same old question:
how can you be free?
I see you cleaning your pipe
with the hairpin
of somebody's innocent night.
I see the plastic Evil Eye
pinned to your underwear.
Once again you throw the pennies,
once again you read
how the pieces of the world
have changed around your question.
Did you get to the Himalayas?
Did you visit that monk in New Jersey?
I never answered any of your letters.
Oh Steve, do you remember me?

1963

TWO WENT TO SLEEP

Two went to sleep
almost every night
one dreamed of mud
one dreamed of Asia
visiting a zeppelin
visiting Nijinsky
Two went to sleep
one dreamed of ribs
one dreamed of senators
Two went to sleep
two travellers
The long marriage
in the dark
The sleep was old
the travellers were old
one dreamed of oranges
one dreamed of Carthage
Two friends asleep
years locked in travel
Good night my darling
as the dreams waved goodbye
one travelled lightly
one walked through water
visiting a chess game
visiting a booth
always returning
to wait out the day
One carried matches
one climbed a beehive
one sold an earphone
one shot a German

Two went to sleep
every sleep went together
wandering away
from an operating table
one dreamed of grass
one dreamed of spokes
one bargained nicely
one was a snowman
one counted medicine
one tasted pencils
one was a child
one was a traitor
visiting heavy industry
visiting the family
Two went to sleep
none could foretell
one went with baskets
one took a ledger
one night happy
one night in terror
Love could not bind them
Fear could not either
they went unconnected
they never knew where
always returning
to wait out the day
parting with kissing
parting with yawns
visiting Death till
they wore out their welcome
visiting Death till
the right disguise worked

1964

FOUND ONCE AGAIN SHAMELESSLY
IGNORING THE SWANS . . .

Found once again shamelessly ignoring the swans who in-
flame the spectators on the shores of American rivers; found
once again allowing the juicy contract to expire because the
telephone has a magic correspondence with my tapeworm;
found once again leaving the garlanded manhood in danger
of long official repose while it is groomed for marble in
seedily historic back rooms; found once again humiliating
the bank clerk with eye-to-eye wrestling, art dogma, lives
that loaf and stare, and other stage whispers of genius;
found once again the chosen object of heavenly longing
such as can ambush a hermit in a forest with visions of a
busy parking lot; found once again smelling mothball
sweaters, titling home movies, untangling Victorian salmon
rods, fanatically convinced that a world of sporty order is
just around the corner; found once again planning the ideal
lonely year which waits like first flesh love on a calendar of
third choices; found once again hovering like a twine-eating
kite over hands that feed me, verbose under the influence
of astrology; found one again selling out to accessible local
purity while Pentagon Tiffany evil alone can guarantee my
power; found once again trusting that my friends grew up
in Eden and will not harm me when at last I am armourless
and absolutely silent; found once again at the very beginning, veteran of several useless ordeals, prophetic but not
seminal, the purist for the masses of tomorrow; found once
again sweetening life which I have abandoned, like a fired
zoo-keeper sneaking peanuts to publicized sodomized ele-
phants; found once again flaunting the rainbow which
demonstrates that I am permitted only that which I urgently
need; found once again cleansing my tongue of all possibilities, of all possibilities but my perfect one.

1964

HE WAS LAME

He was lame
as a 3 legged dog
screamed as he came
through the fog

If you are the Light
give me a light
buddy

1965

I AM TOO LOUD WHEN YOU ARE GONE

I am too loud when you are gone
I am John the Baptist, cheated by mere water
and merciful love, wild but over-known
John of honey, of time, longing not for
music, longing, longing to be Him
I am diminished, I peddle versions of Word
that don't survive the tablets broken stone
I am alone when you are gone

SNOW IS FALLING

Snow is falling.
There is a nude in my room.
She surveys the wine-coloured carpet.

She is eighteen.
She has straight hair.
She speaks no Montreal language.

She doesn't feel like sitting down.
She shows no gooseflesh.
We can hear the storm.

She is lighting a cigarette
from the gas range.
She holds back her long hair.

1958

CLAIM ME, BLOOD, IF YOU
HAVE A STORY

Claim me, blood, if you have a story
to tell with my Jewish face,
you are strong and holy still, only
speak, like the Zohar, of a carved-out place
into which I must pour myself like wine,
an emptiness of history which I must seize
and occupy, calm and full in this confine,
becoming clear "like good wine on its lees."

1965

IN ALMOND TREES LEMON TREES

In almond trees lemon trees
wind and sun do as they please
Butterflies and laundry flutter
My love her hair is blond as butter

Wasps with yellow whiskers wait
for food beside her china plate
Ants beside her little feet
are there to share what she will eat

Who chopped down the bells that say
the world is born again today
We will feed you all my dears
this morning or in later years

SUZANNE TAKES YOU DOWN

Suzanne takes you down
to her place near the river,
you can hear the boats go by
you can stay the night beside her.
And you know that she's half crazy
but that's why you want to be there
and she feeds you tea and oranges
that come all the way from China.
Just when you mean to tell her
that you have no gifts to give her,
she gets you on her wave-length
and she lets the river answer
that you've always been her lover.
     And you want to travel with her,
     you want to travel blind
     and you know that she can trust you
     because you've touched her perfect body
     with your mind.

Jesus was a sailor
when he walked upon the water
and he spent a long time watching
from a lonely wooden tower
and when he knew for certain
only drowning men could see him
he said All men will be sailors then
until the sea shall free them,
but he himself was broken
long before the sky would open,
forsaken, almost human,
he sank beneath your wisdom like a stone.
     And you want to travel with him,

you want to travel blind
and you think maybe you'll trust him
because he touched your perfect body
with his mind.

Suzanne takes your hand
and she leads you to the river,
she is wearing rags and feathers
from Salvation Army counters.
The sun pours down like honey
on our lady of the harbour
as she shows you where to look
among the garbage and the flowers,
there are heroes in the seaweed
there are children in the morning,
they are leaning out for love
they will lean that way forever
while Suzanne she holds the mirror.
    And you want to travel with her
    and you want to travel blind
    and you're sure that she can find you
    because she's touched her perfect body
    with her mind.

THIS MORNING I WAS DRESSED
BY THE WIND

This morning I was dressed by the wind.
The sky said, close your eyes and run
this happy face into a sundrift.
The forest said, never mind, I am as old
as an emerald, walk into me gossiping.
The village said, I am perfect and intricate,
would you like to start right away?
My darling said, I am washing my hair in the water
we caught last year, it tastes of ⸢tone.
This morning I was dressed by the wind,
it was the middle of September in 1965.

V / New Poems

YOU DO NOT HAVE TO LOVE ME

You do not have to love me
just because
you are all the women
I have ever wanted
I was born to follow you
every night
while I am still
the many men who love you

I meet you at a table
I take your fist between my hands
in a solemn taxi
I wake up alone
my hand on your absence
in Hotel Discipline

I wrote all these songs for you
I burned red and black candles
shaped like a man and a woman
I married the smoke
of two pyramids of sandalwood
I prayed for you
I prayed that you would love me
and that you would not love me

YOU LIVE LIKE A GOD

You live like a god
somewhere behind the names
I have for you,
your body made of nets
my shadow's tangled in,
your voice perfect and imperfect
like oracle petals
in a herd of daisies.
You honour your own god
with mist and avalanche
but all I have
is your religion of no promises
and monuments falling
like stars on a field
where you said you never slept.
Shaping your fingernails
with a razorblade
and reading the work
like a Book of Proverbs
no man will ever write for you,
a discarded membrane
of the voice you use
to wrap your silence in
drifts down the gravity between us,
and some machinery
of our daily life
prints an ordinary question in it
like the Lord's Prayer raised
on a rollered penny.
Even before I begin to answer you
I know you won't be listening.
We're together in a room,

it's an evening in October,
no one is writing our history.
Whoever holds us here in the midst of a Law,
I hear him now
I hear him breathing
as he embroiders gorgeously our simple chains.

THE REASON I WRITE

The reason I write
is to make something
as beautiful as you are

When I'm with you
I want to be the kind of hero
I wanted to be
when I was seven years old
a perfect man
who kills

A PERSON WHO EATS MEAT

A person who eats meat
wants to get his teeth into something
A person who does not eat meat
wants to get his teeth into something else
If these thoughts interest you for even a moment
you are lost

IT'S GOOD TO SIT WITH PEOPLE

It's good to sit with people
   who are up so late
your other homes wash away
and other meals you left
   unfinished on the plate
It's just coffee
   and a piano player's cigarette
and Tim Hardin's song
and the song in your head
   that always makes you wait
I'm thinking of you
     little Frédérique
with your white white skin
and your stories of wealth
    in Normandy
I don't think I ever told you
that I wanted to save the world
watching television
    while we made love
ordering Greek wine and olives for you
while my friend scattered
dollar bills over the head
of the belly-dancer
under the clarinettes of Eighth Avenue
listening to your plans
for an exclusive pet shop in Paris
   Your mother telephoned me
she said I was too old for you
and I agreed
but you came to my room
one morning after a long time
because you said you loved me

From time to time I meet men
who said they gave you money
and some girls have said
that you weren't really a model
Don't they know what it means
to be lonely
lonely for boiled eggs in silver cups
lonely for a large dog
who obeys your voice
lonely for rain in Normandy
seen through leaded windows
lonely for a fast car
lonely for restaurant asparagus
lonely for a simple prince
and an explorer
I'm sure they know
but we are all creatures of envy
we need our stone fingernails
on another's beauty
we demand the hidden love
of everyone we meet
the hidden love not the daily love
    Your breasts are beautiful
warm porcelain taste
of worship and greed
    Your eyes come to me
under the perfect spikes
of imperishable eyelashes
    Your mouth living
on French words
and the soft ashes of your make-up
Only with you
    I did not imitate myself
only with you

I asked for nothing
your long long fingers
deciphering your hair
    your lace blouse
borrowed from a photographer
the bathroom lights
flashing on your new red fingernails
your tall legs at attention
    as I watch you from my bed
while you brush dew
        from the mirror
to work behind the enemy lines
        of your masterpiece
Come to me if you grow old
come to me if you need coffee

DO NOT FORGET OLD FRIENDS

Do not forget old friends
you knew long before I met you
the times I know nothing about
being someone
who lives by himself
and only visits you on a raid

INDEX OF FIRST LINES

A kite is a victim you are sure of,   21
A person who eats meat,   87
As the mist leaves no scar,   37

Claim me, blood, if you have a story,   76
Come back to me,   66
Come, my brothers,   51

Do not forget old friends,   91
During the first pogrom they,   9

Eyes: ...... Medium,   54

Finally I called the people I didn't want to hear from,   50
For your sake I said I will praise the moon,   32
Found once again shamelessly ignoring ...,   72

He was lame,   73
Here we are at the window ...,   69
His pain, unowned, he left,   49
How you murdered your family,   10

I am locked in a very expensive suit,   46
I am sorry that the rich man must go,   61
I am too loud when you are gone,   74
I do not know if the world has lied,   43
I heard of a man,   16
I see you on a Greek mattress,   70
I want your warm body to disappear,   56
I was the last passenger of the day,   55
I would like to remind,   60
If I had a shining head,   8
If this looks like a poem,   34
If your neighbor disappears,   17
In almond trees lemon trees,   77
It's good to sit with people,   88
It swings, Jocko,   28

Martha they say you are gentle,   47
My lady was found mutilated,   14

Queen Victoria,   57

Snow is falling,   75
Suzanne takes you down,   78

The big world will find out,   65
The day wasn't exactly my own,   44
The flowers that I left in the ground,   22
The naked weeping girl,   6
The pain-monger came home,   53
The reason I write,   86
There are some men,   25
This morning I was dressed by the wind,   80
Those unshadowed figures, rounded lines of men,   3
Toronto has been good to me,   59
Towering black nuns frighten us,   12
Two went to sleep,   71

Under her grandmother's patchwork quilt,   38

Whatever cities are brought down,   26
When this American woman,   5
When you kneel below me,   36
With Annie gone,   40

You dance on the day you saved,   64
You do not have to love me,   83
You have the lovers,   30
You live like a god,   84
You tell me that silence,   24